Spooky MATH

Count to Add with Baron von Madd

by Spencer Brinker

Consultant:
Kimberly Brenneman, PhD
National Institute for Early Education Research
Rutgers University
New Brunswick, New Jersey

BEARPORT PUBLISHING

New York, New York

Credits

Publisher: Kenn Goin
Senior Editor: Joyce Tavolacci
Creative Director: Spencer Brinker
Photo Illustrations: Kim Jones

Library of Congress Cataloging-in-Publication Data

Brinker, Spencer, author.
 Count to add with Baron Von Madd / by Spencer Brinker ; consultant, Kimberly
Brenneman, PhD, National Institute for Early Education Research, Rutgers University New
Brunswick, New Jersey.
     pages cm. — (Spooky math)
 Audience: Ages 4–9.
 ISBN 978-1-62724-867-9 (library binding) — ISBN 1-62724-867-6 (library binding)
 1. Counting—Juvenile literature. 2. Arithmetic—Juvenile literature. I. Title. II. Series:
Brinker, Spencer. Spooky math.
 QA113.B68724 2016
 513.2'11—dc23

MAR 29 2016

                              2015011928

For more information, write to Bearport Publishing Company, Inc., 45 West 21st Street, Suite 3B, New York, New York 10010. Printed in the United States of America.

10 9 8 7 6 5 4 3 2 1

Contents

Count to Add

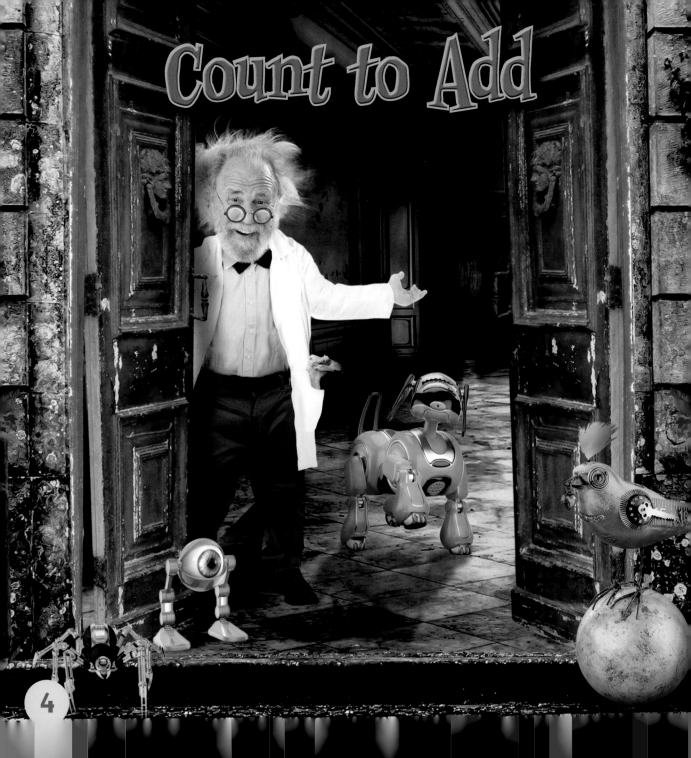

Welcome, young friends!
I'm Baron von Madd.

Some think I'm quite crazy.
I love counting to add!

Step into my lab.
Take a good look around.

Together we'll add up
some things that I've found.

6

How do we add numbers?
Where do the answers
come from?

One way is to count
to find out the sum.

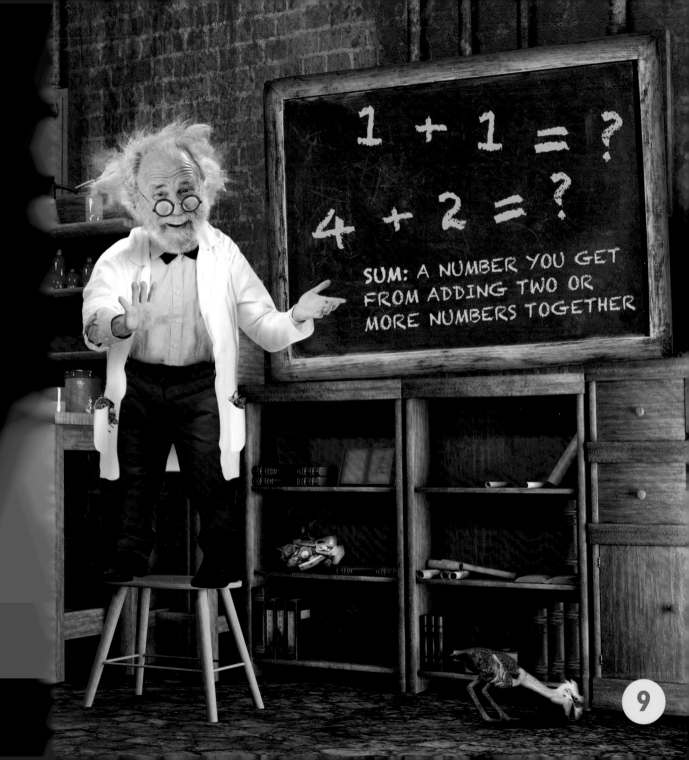

1 + 1 = ?

4 + 2 = ?

SUM: A NUMBER YOU GET FROM ADDING TWO OR MORE NUMBERS TOGETHER

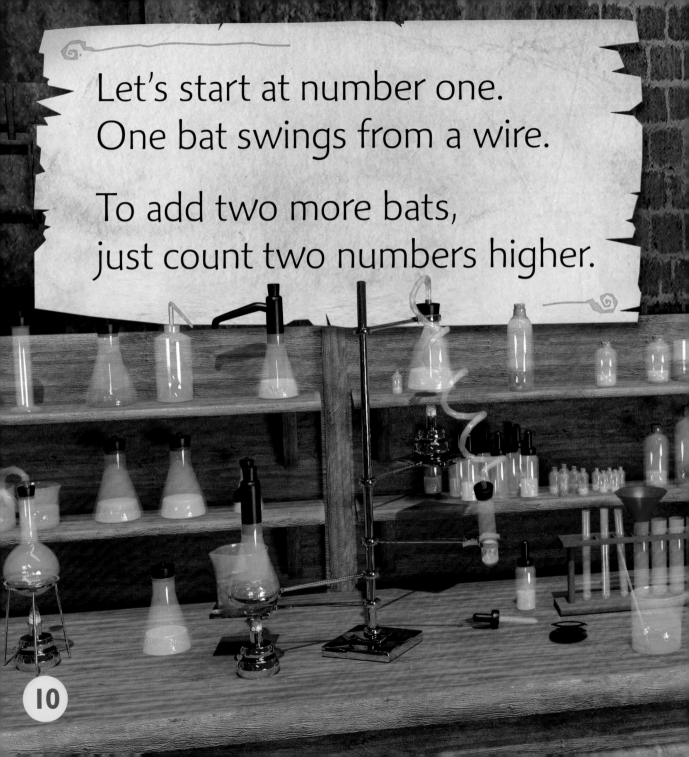

Let's start at number one.
One bat swings from a wire.

To add two more bats,
just count two numbers higher.

$$1 + 2 = \boxed{?}$$

ANSWER: Start with 1, then count 2 more (2, 3). So, 1 + 2 = 3.

The answer stays the same if you flip the numbers around.

Find two bats and add one more. How many have you found?

$2 + 1 = \boxed{?}$

ANSWER: Start with 2, then count 1 more (3). So, 2 + 1 = 3.
2 + 1 = 3 is the same as 1 + 2 = 3.

Let's add larger numbers.
Try this, if you dare.

Start with the bigger number,
and count up from there.

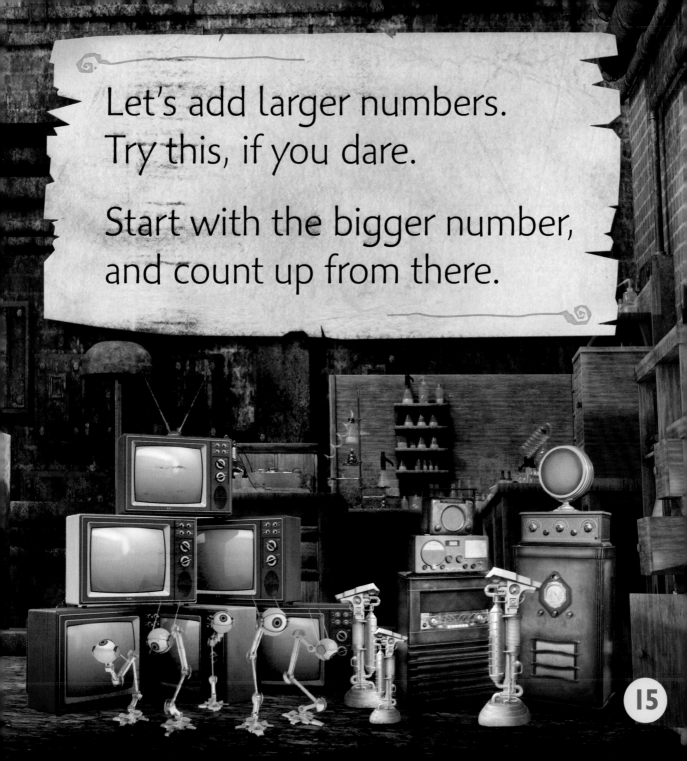

These two slugs are neat. Don't you agree?

If two slugs meet six friends, how many will there be?

$$2 + 6 = \boxed{?}$$

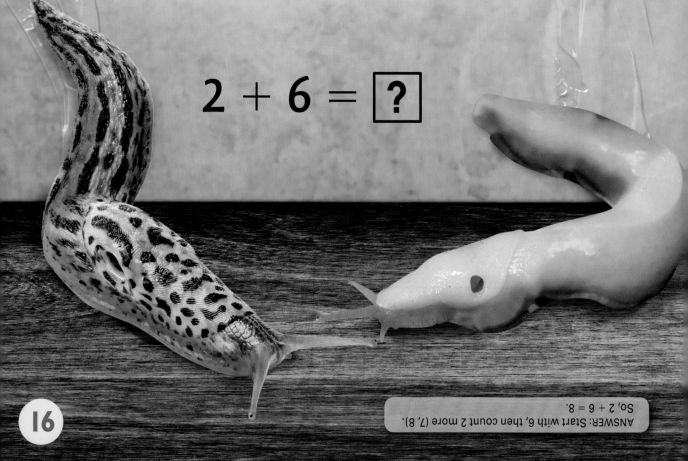

ANSWER: Start with 6, then count 2 more (7, 8). So, 2 + 6 = 8.

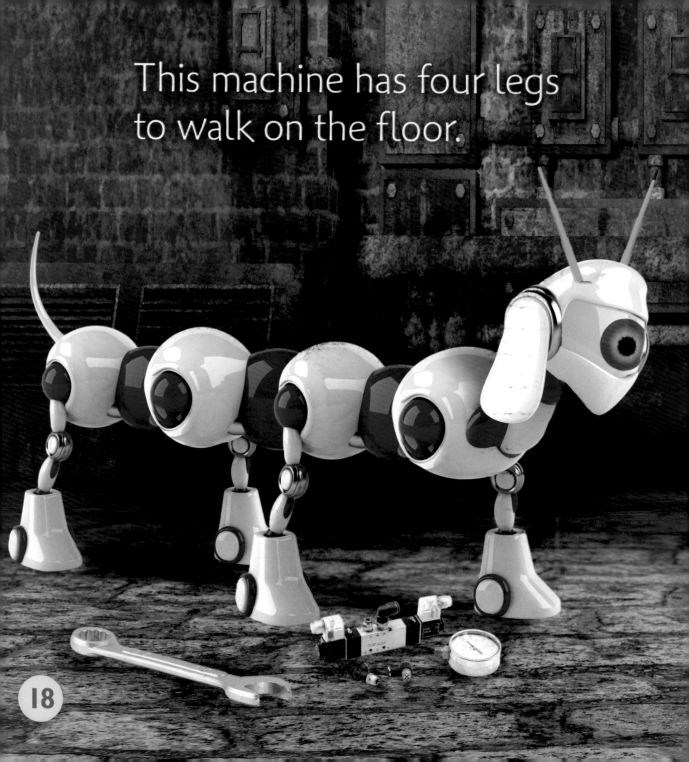

This machine has four legs
to walk on the floor.

18

How many legs will it have
if you add on four more?

$4 + 4 = \boxed{?}$

EXTRA LEGS

19

How many sea creatures
will be on my plate?

I'm going to add seven.
I already have eight.

$$8 + 7 = \boxed{?}$$

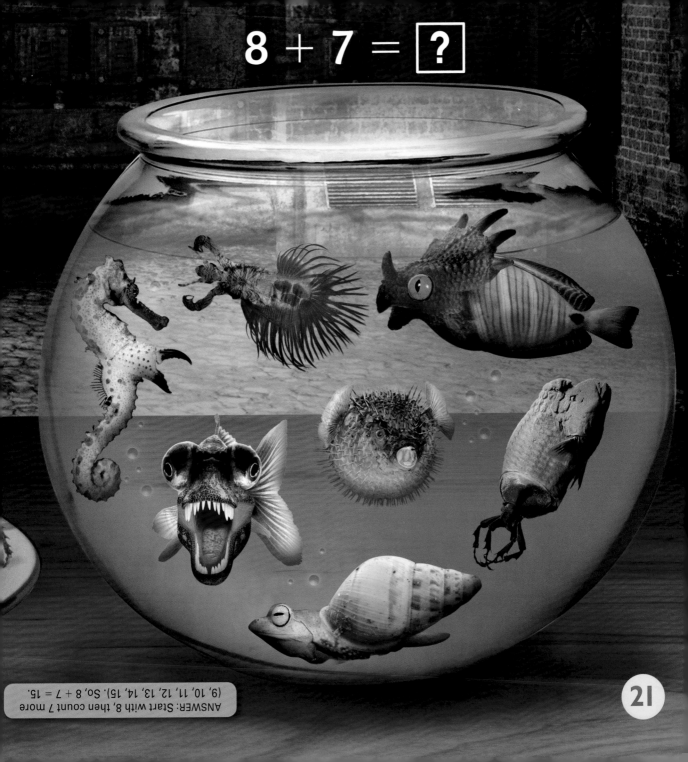

This hat has five bulbs.
It shines very bright.

If I add on twelve more,
I'll have plenty of light.

$5 + 12 = \boxed{?}$

ANSWER: Start with 12, then count 5 more (13, 14, 15, 16, 17). So, 5 + 12 = 17.

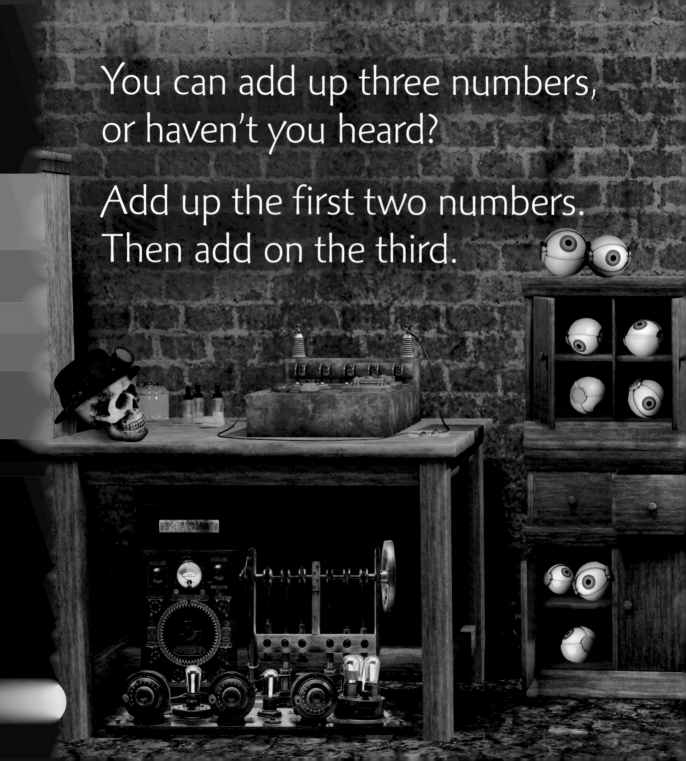

You can add up three numbers,
or haven't you heard?

Add up the first two numbers.
Then add on the third.

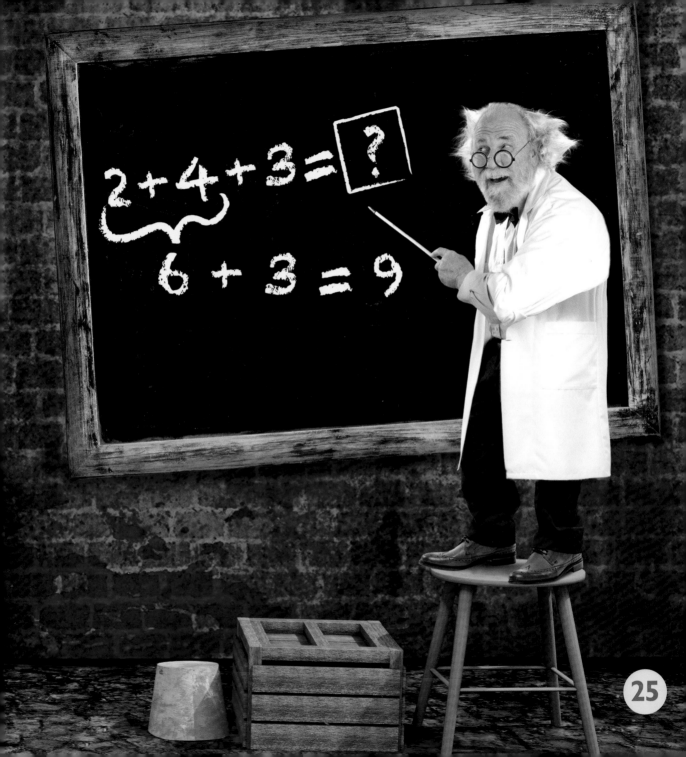

Here are two birds.

Add on four
from my knee.

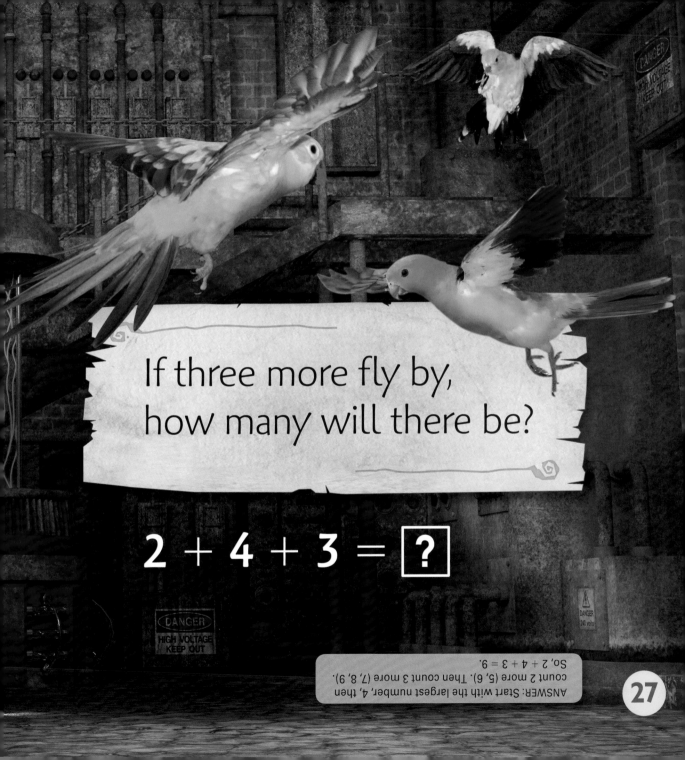

If three more fly by,
how many will there be?

$$2 + 4 + 3 = \boxed{?}$$

I have six small test tubes.
Add four more that are tall.

Add two more with worms.
How many in all?

$$6 + 4 + 2 = \boxed{?}$$

ANSWER: Start with the largest number, 6, then count 4 more (7, 8, 9, 10). Then count 2 more (11, 12).
So, 6 + 4 + 2 = 12.

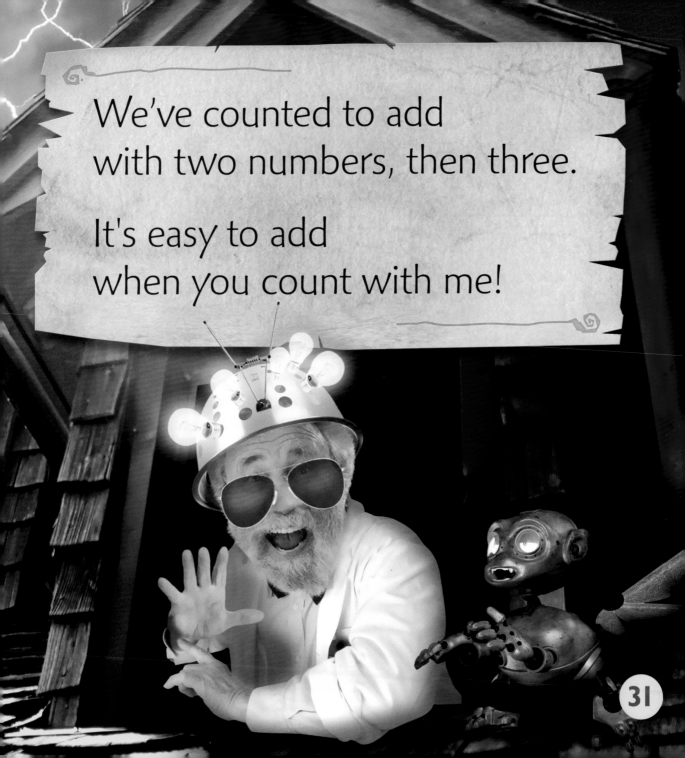

We've counted to add
with two numbers, then three.

It's easy to add
when you count with me!

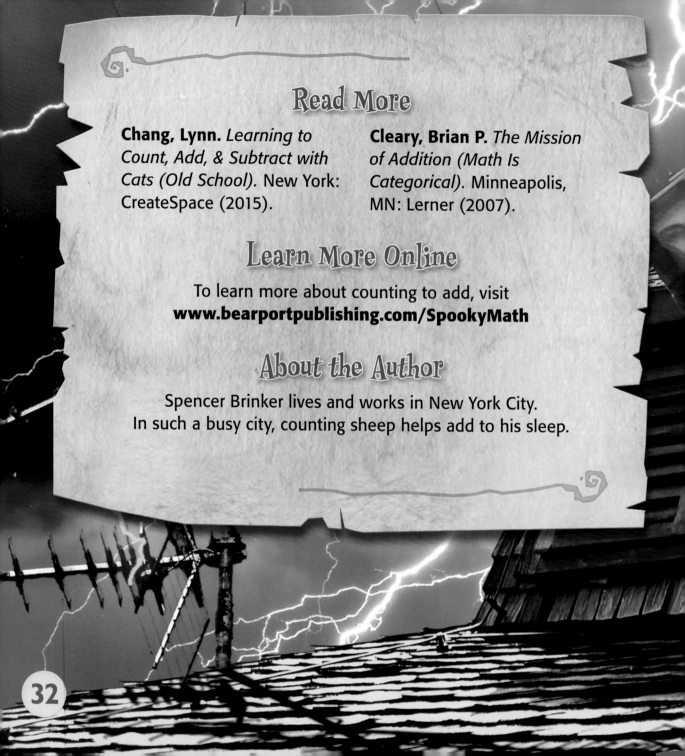

Read More

Chang, Lynn. *Learning to Count, Add, & Subtract with Cats (Old School).* New York: CreateSpace (2015).

Cleary, Brian P. *The Mission of Addition (Math Is Categorical).* Minneapolis, MN: Lerner (2007).

Learn More Online

To learn more about counting to add, visit **www.bearportpublishing.com/SpookyMath**

About the Author

Spencer Brinker lives and works in New York City. In such a busy city, counting sheep helps add to his sleep.